NEW ZEALAND
LANDMARKS

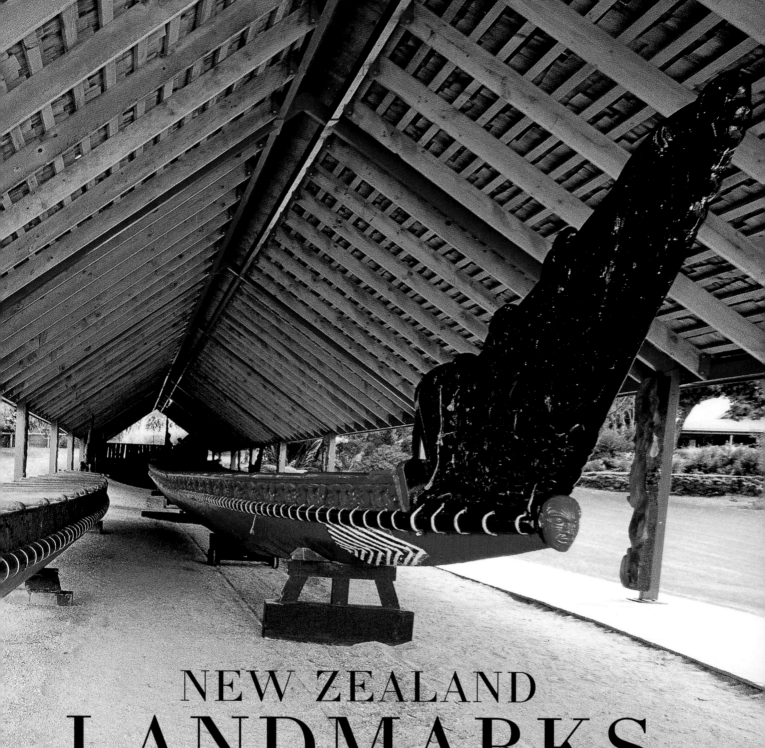

NEW ZEALAND
LANDMARKS

PHOTOGRAPHY BY ROB SUISTED
TEXT BY COLIN MOORE

NH
NEW
HOLLAND

New Zealand

North Island

Cape Reinga
Cape Maria van Diemen
Ninety Mile Beach
Bay of Islands
Kerikeri
Cape Brett
Kawakawa

Whangarei

Leigh
Hauraki Gulf
Waitakere Ranges
AUCKLAND
Coromandel Peninsula
Thames
Paeroa
White Island
Katikati
Mt Maunganui
Te Kaha
East Cape
Tauranga
Te Puke
Opotiki
Hamilton
Whakatane
Tirau
Rotorua
Waitomo
Waiotapu
▲ Mt Tarawera
Tolaga Bay
Wairakei
Whangara
Taupo
Gisborne
Lake Taupo

Tongaporutu
▲ Mt Tongariro
New Plymouth
▲ Mt Ngauruhoe
▲ Mt Ruapehu
Napier
Taranaki/Mt Egmont ▲
Ohakune
Cape Kidnappers
Jerusalem
Waiouru

Wanganui

Palmerston North

South Island

Farewell Spit
Golden Bay
Kapiti Island
Masterton
Castlepoint
Collingwood
Marlborough Sounds
Greytown
Takaka
Martinborough
Tasman Bay
WELLINGTON
Picton
Nelson
Rimutaka Range
Blenheim
Cook Strait
Ngawi
Cape Palliser

Westport
Buller

Punakaiki
Kaikoura

Greymouth
Hanmer Springs
Hokitika

Southern Alps
CHRISTCHURCH
Lyttelton Harbour
Fox Glacier
Banks Peninsula
Mt Tasman ▲
Akaroa Harbour
Aoraki/Mt Cook ▲
Lake Tekapo
Lake Pukaki
Geraldine
Mackenzie Country

Milford Sound
Oamaru

Wanaka
Cromwell
Queenstown
Moeraki
Clyde

Te Anau
Lake Wakatipu

DUNEDIN

Invercargill
The Catlins
Bluff

Stewart Island

INTRODUCTION

Landmarks are conspicuous objects in the landscape, forms and shapes that our eye is drawn to, and that often hold our gaze. From the lighthouse at Cape Reinga in the far north, to a road sign at Bluff at the most southerly end of State Highway 1, New Zealand is a country of landmarks, both natural or fashioned by its inhabitants.

The most obvious and enduring landmarks are geological features that are the visible results of hidden, slow or long-finished processes: the mountains uplifted due to tectonic plate collision, the glaciers fed by the snow from these mountains, the rivers cascading from them depositing their stone to form wide plains, or carrying their sediment to the sea. Uplift and sedimentation create the mountains and plains, water and wind shape the coast, build beaches and carve bays, coves, cliffs, stacks, arches and headlands.

New Zealand is a relatively new landmass. Between 600 and 380 million years ago much of it arose as a row of volcanoes off the edge of the supercontinent of Gondwanaland. After various phases of volcanism and sedimentation, plate collision and uplift, the break-up of the New Zealand edge of Gondwanaland began – New Zealand was set adrift to begin a journey out into the Pacific Ocean.

By some 60 million years ago the journey slowed, with the Tasman Sea separating New Zealand from the Australian edge of the supercontinent left behind. New Zealand was now a group of islands in a shallow sea, one of the most isolated landmasses of its size in the world.

The processes that formed the country continue to shape it today, providing some of its most dramatic natural landmarks. Plate collision continues to push up the Southern Alps as well as providing fire for the central North Island volcanoes. The country is being slowly pushed up or dragged down.

New Zealand carried with it remnants of its Gondwanaland heritage, such as ferns and tuatara, but its long isolation in the South Pacific meant it developed a distinctive and unique flora and fauna. Mostly, it was a land of forests and birds, some of which developed in the absence of mammalian predators and so did not have much need for flight.

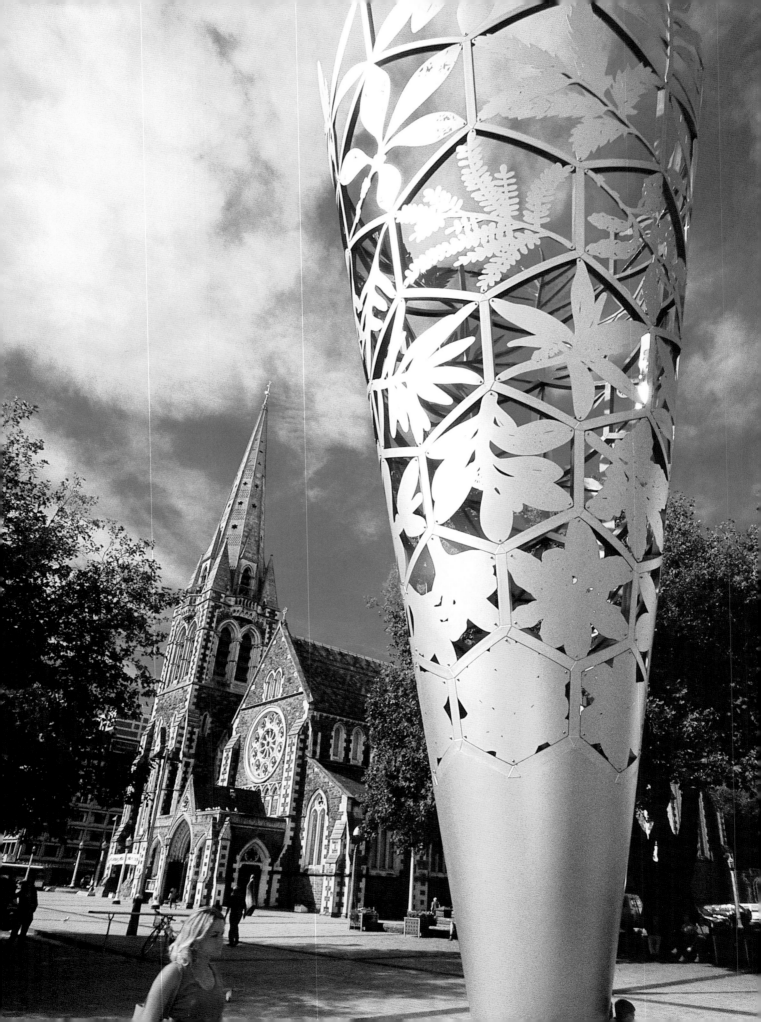

The most obvious and enduring landmarks are geological features that are the visible results of hidden, slow or long-finished processes: the mountains uplifted due to tectonic plate collision, the glaciers fed by the snow from these mountains, the rivers cascading from them depositing their stone to form wide plains, or carrying their sediment to the sea. Uplift and sedimentation create the mountains and plains, water and wind shape the coast, build beaches and carve bays, coves, cliffs, stacks, arches and headlands.

New Zealand is a relatively new landmass. Between 600 and 380 million years ago much of it arose as a row of volcanoes off the edge of the supercontinent of Gondwanaland. After various phases of volcanism and sedimentation, plate collision and uplift, the break-up of the New Zealand edge of Gondwanaland began – New Zealand was set adrift to begin a journey out into the Pacific Ocean. By some 60 million years ago the journey slowed, with the Tasman Sea separating New Zealand from the Australian edge of the supercontinent left behind. New Zealand was now a group of islands in a shallow sea, one of the most isolated landmasses of its size in the world.

The processes that formed the country continue to shape it today, providing some of its most dramatic natural landmarks. Plate collision continues to push up the Southern Alps as well as providing fire for the central North Island volcanoes. The country is being slowly pushed up or dragged down.

New Zealand carried with it remnants of its Gondwanaland heritage, such as ferns and tuatara, but its long isolation in the South Pacific meant it developed a distinctive and unique flora and fauna. Mostly, it was a land of forests and birds, some of which developed in the absence of mammalian predators and so did not have much need for flight.

New Zealand is also young in human terms, being one of the last landmasses of any size to be populated. Polynesian forebears of the Maori first arrived in this land of birds, with its pristine and untouched landscape, around 800 to 1000 years ago, journeying in canoes from eastern Polynesia. They explained nature's art with an imaginative mythology. Islands and peninsulas, mountains and rivers are often the landmarks of the past battles of gods, monsters and men. The tortured landscape of the North Island, a giant fish caught by a young god, carries the scars of knife wounds inflicted on the catch by the god's jealous brothers.

THE NORTH

ISLAND

Previous page TONGARIRO NATIONAL PARK

The Tongariro National Park, listed as a World Heritage Area, offers the 'best one day hike in New Zealand', taking in craters, active volcanoes, mountain springs, emerald lakes and mounds of volcanic rock. This view over Mt Tongariro, from Mt Ngauruhoe encompasses the south crater and blue lake.

Above and right CAPE REINGA

The second most northern spot in New Zealand – North Cape is about 5 kilometres further north – has fortunately retained its Maori name. Te Reinga, the place of leaping, is where the spirits depart from New Zealand for Hawaiiki, the spiritual home of the Maori people and their mythical place of origin. A pohutukawa tree, at least 800 years old, grows out of the rocks at the foot of the cape and the spirits slide down its roots into the sea to begin their journey in the underworld.

Cape Reinga Lighthouse, which is visited by thousands of tourists every year, was built in 1941 using the lens of a light installed on nearby Motuopao Island in 1879. The 1000-watt light bulb is visible 49 kilometres out to sea. Just west of Cape Reinga, the currents of the Tasman Sea and Pacific Ocean meet in a foaming swell of broken water over the Columbia Bank.

Right TE PAKI FARM PARK
Giant sand dunes flank the misnamed Ninety Mile Beach on the west coast of the Aupouri Peninsula, which forms Te Hiku o te Ika (the tail of the fish of Maui). In fact the rollers of the Tasman Sea break onto about 90 kilometres of beach. Some 23,000 hectares of the peninsula, including most of its northern tip, are in the publicly owned Te Paki Farm Park. Tour buses that traverse Ninety Mile Beach to reach Cape Reinga stop near Te Paki Stream so that tourists can 'surf' the dunes.

Below CAPE MARIA VAN DIEMEN
In 1642 Dutch explorer Abel Tasman, the first European to sight New Zealand, named the cape to the west of Te Reinga after the Governor of Batavia's wife. The wide sweep of Te Werahi Beach is a mystical place; here and there the wind sweeps away dune sands to expose the broken shells and oven stones of ancient middens. Motuopao Island is a nature reserve, valued for its breeding colonies of fairy prion, white-faced storm petrel and black-winged petrel.

Right RUAPEKAPEKA PA

In an important early battle of the wars that soon followed European settlement in New Zealand, the Ngapuhi chief Kawiti bloodied the nose of British troops at the pa (fortified village) at Ruapekapeka, south of Kawakawa. Kawiti built his fortress with skilfully angled trenches and massive earthen ramparts on inland heights where he could watch the approach of British soldiers from the Bay of Islands 30 kilometres away. It took 23 days for the 1100 British troops under Colonel Despard to haul three 32-pounder cannon, one 18-pounder, two 12-pound howitzers, one 6-pounder, four mortars and two rocket tubes to the pa. The defensive earthworks, some of which are still visible, were similar to those to be used later in the First World War. They withstood the assault until the British troops managed to storm Ruapekapeka on a Sunday while most of the defenders were at the rear of the pa, engaged in prayer.

Above MEETING HOUSE, WAITANGI

On these historic grounds, now a national reserve, the modern nation of New Zealand was forged in a compact between Maori and the British Crown. The Whare Runanga (meeting house) at Waitangi was completed in 1940 to mark the centenary of the signing of the Treaty of Waitangi by Captain William Hobson, representing the British Crown, and 45 Maori chiefs.

Below WAITANGI GROUNDS

The Treaty flagstaff at the Waitangi National Reserve marks the spot where the Treaty of Waitangi was signed on 6 February 1840. The treaty promised Maori possession of their lands and resources and all the rights of British subjects in exchange for ceding sovereignty to the Crown. In recent years the flagstaff has been the scene of protest by Maori activists who believe the treaty has not been upheld.

Above HOLE IN THE ROCK, PIERCY ISLAND

Named by Captain James Cook for the over 150 islands that are embraced within 800 kilometres of irregular northern coastline, the Bay of Islands is the cradle of New Zealand history for Maori and Pakeha. Some islands are privately owned but several are contained within the Bay of Islands Maritime and Historic Park. Among the most famous is Piercy Island just beyond Cape Brett on the southern extremity of the Bay of Islands. Here, tour boats, large and small, sail through the Hole in the Rock. The deep waters are rich in pelagic game fish.

Below **PUBLIC TOILETS, KAWAKAWA**
Kawakawa, a stagnant former coal-mining town known only for the railway line that runs through its main street, was given a new lease of life by the renowned Austrian artist and architect, Frederick Hundertwasser. The town's world famous public toilets were designed by Hundertwasser, who settled near Kawakawa in 1975. The artist died in February 2000 and is buried near the town he revived.

Above **STONE STORE, KERIKERI**
The stone store in the Kerikeri Basin at the head of the Kerikeri Inlet was built by missionaries in 1833 to protect their supplies from Maori attack. It is the oldest stone building in New Zealand and still serves as a shop, with a museum upstairs. Kemp House, next to the stone store, was built for the English missionary James Kemp in 1822 and is the oldest surviving house in New Zealand. The buildings are fully protected as historic places.

Left and right **KAURI**
Giant kauri trees (Agathis australis), such as these in the Puketi Forest near Kerikeri, were coveted by the British navy of the 19th century to use as spars for its battleships. After European settlement the prized timber was mercilessly logged. Those at Puketi, one of the last places where kauri was milled, were saved by the discovery of a breeding population of the rare kokako, or blue wattle crow. Tane Mahuta, the largest living kauri, is 'Lord of the Forest' in the 9000-hectare Waipoua Forest Sanctuary. The giant is up to 2000 years old and contains enough timber in its trunk to build 12 three-bedroom weatherboard houses from the floor up.

Above KAWAU ISLAND

The mansion and wharf in Bon Accord Harbour at Kawau Island were built in 1862 by the New Zealand Governor, Sir George Grey. The island in the Hauraki Gulf had previously been the scene of a short-lived copper mining venture. Grey rebuilt the mine manager's house into a mansion and imported a collection of exotic animals such as zebras and kangaroos. Wallabies still roam parts of Kawau. Mansion House was bought by the Government in 1967 and restored.

Right GOAT ISLAND

The marine reserve at Goat Island, near Leigh – officially the Cape Rodney to Okakari Point Marine Reserve – became New Zealand's first marine reserve when it was created in 1977. The coast now teems with fish and underwater life and attracts thousands of snorkellers and divers. Its success has led to the creation of other marine reserves throughout New Zealand.

Left MURIWAI GANNET COLONY
New Zealand's most accessible Australasian
gannet colony is on Otakamiro Point at Muriwai
Beach on Auckland's west coast, where more
than 1200 breeding pairs nest on an old lava
column. The colony, the Takapu Refuge, has
expanded onto two neighbouring cliff-top sites
since the birds first began to breed at Muriwai
in 1975. Young birds spend five to six years in
Australian waters before returning to breed.

Over page PIHA BEACH
Windswept and rugged, the beaches of the
west coast are known for their black iron sands
– mined for ore in some places – and bumper
surf rolling in from the Tasman Sea. Piha
Beach, stretching between Lion Rock and Te
Waha Point in the distance, is an old and
popular Auckland holiday retreat that despite
considerable settlement still retains a wild
atmosphere. It is the venue for many surfing
competitions.

ight WAITAKERE RANGES
he bush-clad Waitakere Ranges are the
ackground to the canvas of metropolitan
uckland. Formed by volcanic activity around
5 million years ago, the ranges were
xtensively logged but now, as parkland and
vater-catchment area, draw nearly three million
isitors a year to regenerating native forests.
here are 140 tracks and 200 kilometres of
rails in the Waitakere Ranges Regional Park,
vith lookouts that give views over both the
Manukau and Waitemata harbours.

Above VIADUCT HARBOUR

An old fishing harbour in Auckland was revitalised for New Zealand's first defence of the America's Cup in 2000. Cafés and apartments were built around berths for super-yachts and the bases of challenging syndicates. The area was developed further for the 2003 regatta when the Swiss challenger Alinghi wrested the 'Auld Mug' from Team New Zealand. The Viaduct Harbour remains as a permanent legacy of New Zealand's eight-year tenure as holders of yachting's oldest trophy.

Right SKY TOWER AND TOWN HALL

Auckland city's newest landmark building, Sky Tower, and one of its oldest, the Auckland Town Hall clock tower, brighten the night sky. The civic hall, with a base of Melbourne bluestone and facades of Oamaru stone, was opened in December 1911. It has variously housed the municipal offices and Council Chamber, and includes a great hall, a smaller concert chamber and a large pipe organ. For many years it was the city's only concert theatre and is still used regularly as a concert venue.

Right ONE TREE HILL

Some 2000 Maori once lived on the extensive terracing and fortifications of One Tree Hill or Maungakiekie, a volcano that erupted 20,000 years ago. The village was the home of the region's most famous early chief, Kiwi Tamaki of the Waiohua, until his tribe was driven from its stronghold by the Ngati Whatua in about 1750. The abandoned land was bought by Sir John Logan Campbell in the 19th century, who gifted it to the public in 1901. Campbell planted a group of pines on the 183-metre summit to protect some natives trees that he intended would replace a lone sacred totara tree, which had grown there until the 1850s. Only one pine survived – until it was destroyed by Maori activists in 1999. Campbell was buried on the summit in 1912; a 21-metre obelisk is his memorial to the Maori people.

Right RANGITOTO

Auckland's most famous visual icon is the youngest of the 48 volcanoes in the region. The island erupted around 600 years ago and was witnessed by Maori living on neighbouring Motutapu Island. Rangitoto means 'bloody sky' but the name actually refers to the wounds of a battle on the island, rather than to the eruption. In an amazing display of nature's handiwork the bare basaltic lava of Rangitoto was colonised by pohutukawa trees and now hosts more than 200 different plant species. The island is a public park with walking tracks to its 259-metre summit.

Below **CITY BUILDINGS**
Greater Auckland is New Zealand's largest city, with more than one million residents. It is also the commercial capital with many of the country's largest companies having their head offices in Auckland's office tower blocks. A recent addition to the skyline is the Sky City Casino and its landmark Sky Tower. At 328 metres, the Tower is New Zealand's tallest structure, and includes an observation platform and revolving restaurant.

Above **AUCKLAND BY NIGHT**
Thousands of commuters pour into Auckland's Central Business District every day, most in private cars, providing a major and worrying source of congestion. By night the CBD remains popular for its restaurants and clubs. A greater variety of nightlife and eateries has followed the relatively recent arrival of apartment complexes to the centre of the city.

Left AUCKLAND HARBOUR BRIDGE
Since its completion in 1959, the 'coathanger'
bridge across the Waitemata Harbour has
opened up the North Shore, once a holiday
destination, into the fastest-growing region in
New Zealand. The suburban explosion was so
great that in the late 1960s the bridge capacity
had to be doubled with the innovative addition
of two lanes 'clipped on' to both sides of the
bridge. The bridge also has a moveable central
barrier that is relocated before rush hour to aid
the flow of the more than 160,000 vehicles that
cross the harbour daily. Auckland, where one in
every four households owns a boat, is known
as the City of Sails and the Waitemata boasts
one of the world's largest one-day regattas.

Left **LOST WORLD CAVE**
A 100-metre free-hanging abseil – the
equivalent of descending 30 storeys –
precedes a three-hour journey through the
misty Lost World Cave. The cave, discovered in
1906, is one of many in the Waitomo district.
The caves are mostly noted for their ethereal,
Milky Way display of glow-worms. The worms,
the larvae of the fungus gnat, produce a soft
greenish light that attracts unwary insects to
become entangled in a string of sticky threads,
lowered by the glow-worm from its web. The
glow-worm then reels in the thread and
consumes its prey.

Below **CATHERWOOD'S CAVE**
The limestone caves that riddle the Waitomo
region are filled with the stalactite and
stalagmite sculptures of nature as well as flow
stone and cave coral as found in Catherwood's
Cave. As well as being a magnet for tourists
the Waitomo complex draws ardent
speleologists to their secret and beautiful inner
chambers.

Left **BRIDAL VEIL FALLS**
After its 55-metre plunge the Pakoka River seems to disappear, which prompted Maori to describe the falls evocatively as the Water of the Underworld. The falls are in a 200-hectare scenic reserve south of Raglan, a west coast beach resort famed for its surf breaks.

Right **DAIRY COWS, WAIKATO**
Dairying accounts for 20 per cent of New Zealand's export income and the undisputed centre of the industry is the lush grasslands of the Waikato. The region's representative rugby team has a 'Mooloo' mascot and fans ring cowbells in support of their team. In 2002 there were 3.3 million milking cows in New Zealand on 13,900 dairy farms, producing 13 billion litres of milk. The average herd size is 251 and many farmers milk more than 500 cows twice daily.

Above HAMILTON GARDENS

A 58-hectare site alongside the Waikato River that was once the dusty wasteland of an old stock car racing track has been transformed into a series of beautiful themed gardens. The gardening projects are managed by 15 voluntary trusts. In all, there are 100 different garden themes, including several Japanese traditions and Chinese from various dynasties. The traditional Italian Renaissance garden is laid out in a grid pattern, based on a design that seeks to rationalise and collect nature in the tradition of the time.

Right WAIKATO RIVER

New Zealand's longest river, the Waikato, flows through Hamilton, the country's fifth largest city, on its 425-kilometre journey from Lake Taupo to the Tasman Sea. The river has previously been a major highway for Maori and early Pakeha settlers and is now, through a series of dams, an important source of hydro-electricity. In Hamilton the river is used extensively for recreation.

Left **L&P BOTTLE STATUE, PAEROA**
The pleasant small township of Paeroa began as an inland port on the Waihou River and service centre for the nearby Karangahake Gorge goldfields. But to most people the town is known for a bottled soft drink with the essential ingredient of mineral water from a Paeroa spring. Lemon and Paeroa (L&P), with its distinctive taste, is still produced, although not in Paeroa but the town, as popular L&P advertising proclaims, remains 'world famous in New Zealand'.

Below **BIG SHEEP AND SHEEPDOG, TIRAU**
Tirau, once known as Oxford, had all but disappeared until reinventing itself as a town of antique and collectible shops. The town is strategically located on State Highway 1 to catch travellers and tourists heading for Rotorua and Taupo. The giant sheep is a corrugated iron building housing a shop selling New Zealand souvenirs. The sheepdog building contains a tourist information centre.

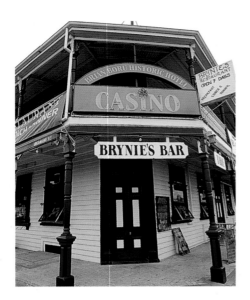

Left BRIAN BORU HOTEL, THAMES
When Thames, gateway to the Coromandel, was declared a goldfield in 1867 the population exploded to become bigger than Auckland's and the town boasted more than 100 hotels. The Coromandel gold rush was rich but relatively brief and just four old hotels survive in Thames' main street, notably the Brian Boru, which has been dispensing ale since 1868.

Above HOT WATER BEACH
At Hot Water Beach on the east coast of the Coromandel Peninsula thermal waters bubble just beneath the sand. At low tide bathers can dig their own natural spa – and then retreat to the sea to cool off. Care has to be taken swimming, however, as in places the beach has dangerous currents.

Right CATHEDRAL COVE
The soft sandstone on the Coromandel coast near Mercury Bay has been carved by the wind and tide into evocatively shaped stacks and huge caverns. One arch, admired by Captain Cook when he visited the coast in 1769 and called by early Pakeha the Mare's Leg because of its shape, collapsed into the sea during a violent storm in 1978. Mare's Leg Cove remains, as does neighbouring Cathedral Cove.

Above **LAKE TAUPO**
The snow-capped and steaming mountain trio of the central North Island were confirmed as occupied Maori land when Horonuku Te Heuheu Tukino IV strode to a courtroom window that looked across the expanse of Lake Taupo and thundered, 'Behold my fire [of occupation].' In 1887 the Ngati Tuwharetoa paramount chief gifted his tribe's sacred summits to the nation to become the country's first national park. Lake Taupo, New Zealand's largest lake, fills the crater left by various massive volcanic explosions, the most recent in AD 230.

Right **JET BOAT, HUKA FALLS**
At Huka Falls the Waikato River draining Lake Taupo squeezes through a narrow cleft in the rock to create a short but frightening blast of foaming water. The savage volume of water plunging through the gap has not stopped several kayakers from successfully running the falls. A less frightening way to appreciate the water's power is from the cockpit of a tourist jet boat.

Left BUNGY, WAIKATO RIVER
A 47-metre bungy jump above the Waikato River, near Taupo, is the most popular in the North Island because of its scenic setting. New Zealander A.J. Hackett was the first to commercialise the instant adrenalin rush of diving into space attached to an elastic 'bungy' cord. The thrill has now spread throughout the world but jumps into natural settings are usually far more spectacular than in constructed surroundings.

Over page MT TARAWERA
When Mt Tarawera erupted with devastating violence in 1886 its ash and lava buried the world-famous Victorian-era tourist attraction of the pink and white silica terraces. The nearby Maori villages of Te Ariki, Moura and Te Wairoa were also engulfed by mud and ash, killing 153 people. The buried village at Te Wairoa, where time has stood still since that fateful day, is now a tourist attraction. The brooding mountain's crater creates a 6-kilometre by 250-metre rift through the massif.

Right CRATERS OF THE MOON, WAIRAKEI
The Craters of the Moon steamed into life in the 1950s when the nearby Wairakei Geothermal Power project lowered underground water levels, reducing the pressure of heated water and causing more vigorous boiling and steaming. As a result, new mud pools and steam vents appeared in a previously quiet area. The feature is administered by the Department of Conservation.

Above CHAMPAGNE POOL,
WAIOTAPU

The many-hued sulphur deposits of The Artists
Palette frame the Champagne Pool hot spring
at Waiotapu, south of Rotorua. The thermal
area is best known for the Lady Knox Geyser,
which spouts each day at 10.15 am to the
delight of tourists. The geyser's punctuality is
ensured by blocking the outlet with rags so as
to create increased pressure and then using
soap powder as a catalyst to send the heated
water gushing into the sky.

Right GEYSERS, WHAKAREWAREWA

Te Whakarewarewa, the pre-eminent thermal
area in Rotorua, now bares little resemblance
to the old area where tourists walked between
boiling mud pools under the care of Maori
guides and tossed pennies into a stream for
children to dive for. Under the care of the New
Zealand Maori Arts and Crafts Institute,
'Whaka', as it is still known, is a modern tourist
area with paved paths and electric trains. But
the Prince of Wales Geyser (left) and Pohutu
Geyser, which thunders to a height of more
than 30 metres, remain unchanged.

Left GATEWAY, WHAKAREWAREWA
The Maori Arts and Crafts Institute keeps alive Maori cultural traditions with rigorous and lengthy courses on Maori art where students can learn from recognised masters. Carving is a major Maori art form and the gate to the institute is a tribute to the Romeo and Juliet-style love story of Tutanekai and Hinemoa. In Te Arawa legend the maiden Hinemoa swam across Lake Rotorua to Mokoia Island to join her lover, the young chief Tutanekai.

Below WHITE ISLAND
The Pacific Ring of Fire emerges 50 kilometres off the Bay of Plenty coast in the active volcano of White Island (Whakaari). The smoking and steaming island near Whakatane was once mined for sulphur but abandoned because of mud flows and volcanic activity – although not before 11 miners were killed during an eruption in 1914. The island's sulphuric moonscape is regularly visited by guided tour parties.

Above MT EDGECUMBE

The next New Zealand mountain in the Pacific Ring of Fire is the 821-metre Mt Edgecumbe (Putauaki) on the Rangitaiki Plains. In Maori legend Edgecumbe was banished to the Bay of Plenty after a fight with the mighty Mt Tongariro in the central North Island. Mt Edgecumbe is not active but the land around it has been subjected to violent earthquakes.

Right MT MAUNGANUI

Mariners are unlikely to miss the entrance to Tauranga Harbour and the booming Bay of Plenty port of Mt Maunganui. The 232-metre mountain that guards the harbour entrance is a Tauranga icon. It also flanks Main Beach, one of the country's most famous surf beaches, and is the backdrop to a holiday haven with more than a little resemblance to Australia's famed Surfer's Paradise. Several walking tracks ring Mt Maunganui, which was once an important Maori fortress.

Right BIG KIWIFRUIT, TE PUKE
New Zealand horticulturists took the humble Chinese gooseberry and marketed is so successfully as kiwifruit that the delicacy is now grown throughout the world in competition with those who created its new name. Nonetheless, New Zealand growers still enjoy some seasonal advantage and are generally reckoned to produce the best fruit in the world. A giant kiwifruit fronts a kiwifruit-based tourism venture in the Bay of Plenty town of Te Puke, the heart of kiwifruit-growing country.

Below MURALS, KATIKATI
Small towns find novel ways to spark rebirth. Katikati, another kiwifruit-growing centre in the Bay of Plenty, has reinvented itself as the mural town, a place where the past is portrayed in giant paintings on the walls of its main street buildings. Pride of place is the mural depiction of Irish immigrant George Vesey Stewart, founder of the town in 1875, and brought back to life in 1996 by painter Fee Simon.

Right ANGLICAN CHURCH, RAUKOKERE

The eastern Bay of Plenty and East Coast regions of the North Island share one of New Zealand's most beautiful coastlines, with numerous bays flanked by pohutukawa trees. It is also an area rich in Maori tradition and early European settlement. The Anglican church at Raukokore, west of Orete Point, is a delightful survivor of early missionary endeavour.

Below MAIN STREET, OPOTIKI

Opotiki was once the centre of a hugely prosperous Maori settlement and in the early days of European immigration had a bustling port. The town now survives as a service centre to agriculture and as the western gateway for travellers around the East Cape. This carved pole in the main street is a proud reminder of Opotiki's past, depicting the changes and progress of the district since European settlement.

ght BRIDGE, WAIOEKA GORGE
e inland route from Opotiki to Gisborne
lows the Waioeka River through the Waioeka
orge. The road is narrow in places and has
any turns but the stretch through the
aioeka Gorge Scenic Reserve is one of the
ost idyllic you will find. The reserve is the
gest of its kind in New Zealand and one of
e many walking tracks crosses the Waioeka
ver on an old harp suspension bridge.

ow EASTERN BAY OF PLENTY
e many secluded coves and sandy beaches
ong this coast were once renowned as places
r 'free' summer holiday camping. Landowners
d local authorities no longer allow
lidaymakers to pitch their tents
discriminately but 'The Coast' remains a
pular summer holiday destination.

Above LIGHTHOUSE, EAST CAPE

East Cape lighthouse is the most easterly in the country. Before automation its light keepers were the first New Zealanders to see the sunrise each new day. Since 1990 all 42 lighthouses around the New Zealand coast have been automated and the once uniquely remote lifestyle of the lighthouse keepers and their families has gone.

Above TOLAGA BAY

Captain Cook anchored at Tolaga Bay, north of Gisborne, during his first visit to New Zealand in 1769. On his second voyage 10 years later he again visited the bay to fill the ship's water casks. For most people, however, Tolaga Bay is noted for its wharf, the longest in New Zealand. It was built in the 1920s to serve coastal shipping and commercial fishing boats.

Below MEETING HOUSE, WHANGARA

The tiny and isolated Maori community of Whangara, south of Tolaga Bay, has become famous since Witi Ihimaera's heart-wrenching novel *The Whale Rider,* set in Whangara, became the subject of an international award-winning feature film of the same name. The story is based on the tribe's legendary ancestor Paikea, who can be seen riding a whale in a carving on the roof of the wharenui (meeting house) on the Whangara marae.

Left CLOCK TOWER, GISBORNE

The clock tower monument at the foot of Kaiti Hill in the East Coast city of Gisborne marks the location where Captain James Cook first set foot on New Zealand in October 1769. Nicholas Young, cabin boy on Cook's ship Endeavour, was the first aboard to sight Aotearoa. The promontory near Gisborne, Young Nicks Head, was named by Cook in his honour. Gisborne is the principal city in a region noted for its horticulture and vineyards and, ironically, called Poverty Bay by Cook.

Right THE SPIRIT OF NAPIER
More than 250 people were killed when a massive earthquake hit the Hawke's Bay city of Napier in 1931. The earthquake registered 7.9 on the Richter scale and raised more than 2000 hectares of land from the sea bed. 'The Spirit of Napier' statue and fountain on Napier's Marine Parade celebrates the spirit of the people who rebuilt their city and their lives.

Below A&B BUILDING, NAPIER
The devastating Napier earthquake coincided with an American building fashion that has become known as Art Deco. Many of the homes and public buildings in Napier were rebuilt in the Art Deco style, which has similarities with the architecture of Southern California or Mexico, decorated with bold plaster motifs. Napier now holds Art Deco festivals and draws aficionados from around the world.

Left **TE MATA PEAK**
The 399 metre-high bulk of Te Mata Peak
overlooks Hawke's Bay and the Tukituki River.
There are several walking tracks above and
below the peak's high limestone bluffs that yield
views from the ocean in the east to Mt
Ruapehu far to the west.

Below **GANNETS, CAPE KIDNAPPERS**
Cape Kidnappers was named by Captain Cook
in 1769 when a party of Maori tried to kidnap a
Tahitian member of his crew, perhaps thinking
the Polynesian sailor was an enslaved Maori.
An Australasian gannet colony at the cape is
used by 10,000 breeding pairs who arrive in
late July to nest.

Right PUKEKURA PARK

Few public parks are as delightful as New Plymouth's Pukekura Park. The 49-hectare park, just 10 minutes' walk from the centre of Taranaki's largest city, contains formal flower gardens, bush walks, streams, ponds and a kiosk cafe. There are also houses with orchids and other exotic plants, as well as the most picturesque cricket oval in the country. In the summer various features in the park are decorated and floodlit to create imaginative grottoes and colourful waterfalls.

Right DAWSON FALLS

The Kapuni Stream collects snowmelt from the heights of Mt Taranaki/Egmont until at Dawson Falls it plunges over the 18-metre face of an 1800-year-old lava flow. Maori called the falls Rere-a-Noke, after a warrior who eluded his pursuers by hiding beneath the falls. There are several walks near the falls, as well as a trampers' hut and tourist lodge.

Below LIGHTHOUSE, CAPE EGMONT

The lighthouse at Cape Egmont, near New Plymouth, built in 1881, was automated in 1985. Captain Cook gave the cape, and the region's distinctive mountain, the name Egmont after the Earl of Egmont, who had encouraged his pioneering voyage. Recently the name of the mountain was officially changed to Mt Taranaki/Egmont to incorporate its Maori name.

Left THREE SISTERS
Along the North Taranaki coast near Tongaporutu are the distinctive sandstone pillars of the Three Sisters rocks. North of Tongaporutu the coastal cliffs are adorned in a shrub known as golden tainui, which legend says grew from the timbers of the Tainui canoe, one of the Maori migratory canoes.

Below MT TARANAKI/EGMONT
Ask a child to paint a mountain and the result will be much like the 2518-metre andesite cone that dominates the Taranaki region. Mt Taranaki/Egmont and its smaller outlier, Fanthams Peak, are a favoured destination for hikers and climbers. Seemingly benign, the mountain has claimed more lives than any other in New Zealand because of its exposure to sudden weather change and dangerous ice.

Previous page **MT NGAURUHOE**
When Polynesian explorer and great priest
Ngatoro-i-rangi, fresh from the warmth of
tropical Hawaiiki, climbed to the summit of Mt
Ngauruhoe to spy out the new land, he was
enveloped by a sudden snowstorm. In his
distress at the new experience he cried out to
his priestess sisters in the tropics to send fire to
warm him and to ensure they listened he
sacrificed his female slave Auruhoe. When his
sisters responded with volcanic fire by way of
White Island and Rotorua the grateful Ngatoro
threw Auruhoe's body into the burning crater.

Below **MT NGAURUHOE**
Beyond the Pinnacle Ridge of Mt Ruapehu the
2290-metre andesite cone of Mt Ngauruhoe
continues to smoulder with the fire Ngatoro
called for. Mt Ngauruhoe is the youngest of the
central North Island mountains, beginning life
as a new vent on the eroded southern flanks of
Mt Tongariro. Ngauruhoe is still active and
seems to erupt with spectacular displays of ash
and molten lava about every 10 years.

Above and right **MT RUAPEHU**
A modern promotion for the ski slopes on the
Mt Ruapehu massif dubbed the mountain as
magic. And so it can be at sunset when red
and purple tinge the snow slopes that climb to
2796 metres and the lights come on at the
Grand Chateau, a luxury hotel whose life since
it was built in 1929 has included a stint as a
sanatorium. Mt Ruapehu is the centrepiece of

the Tongariro National Park, a listed World
Heritage area. The mountain erupts with
unforgiving regularity, most recently in 1995-96
The Tama Lakes that lie in the high saddle
between Ruapehu and Ngauruhoe are 10,000-
year-old explosion craters, the oldest in the
park and, according to Maori mythology, were
left when Mt Taranaki was banished to the
west.

Above JERUSALEM

Jerusalem, a Catholic mission settlement
founded on the Whanganui River in 1883,
might well have disappeared into antiquity had
not the eccentric modern poet James K.
Baxter, a convert to Catholicism, established a
commune there in 1969. Pilgrims to Baxter,
missionary endeavour, and the beauty of the
290-kilometre Whanganui River, long a vital
transportation route for Maori and early
European settlers, continue to give praise in
Jerusalem.

Right TANGIWAI MEMORIAL

On 24 December 1953, a wall of ice that held
back the steaming water in the crater of Mt
Ruapehu gave way and a tidal wave of mud
and water surged down the Whangaehu River.
The lahar destroyed the rail bridge at Tangiwai,
near Waiouru, just before the arrival of the
nightly passenger express train from Auckland
to Wellington. The train plunged into the abyss
and 153 people lost their lives.

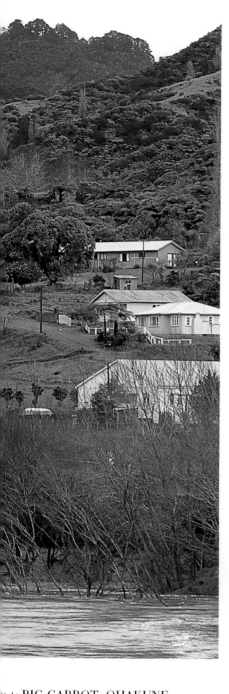

Right **BIG CARROT, OHAKUNE**
If it weren't so cold, rabbits would love the country around Ohakune. Rich volcanic soil and light frosts make the land in the region ideal for growing root crops, particularly carrots. The heart of carrot-growing country is also a vibrant service town for the Turoa skifeld on the southern slopes of Mt Ruapehu.

Left MANGAWEKA

The Rangitikei River is one of the North Island's best rivers for rafting and kayaking. Its headwaters are in the Kaimanawa Ranges and it flows on an almost direct course south-west to the sea through some of the most impressive gorge scenery in New Zealand. Near Mangaweka the river is flanked by massive white siltstone cliffs.

Right MANAWATU GORGE

A few kilometres north of Palmerston North the highway to Napier turns suddenly into the spectacular Manawatu Gorge. The massive crags suggest that the furious Manawatu River has carved a course between the Ruahine Range and the Tararua Range. In fact, the river, which has its headwaters east of the dividing range and its mouth on the west coast, was there before the ranges and its grinding, cutting force has been able to keep pace with the rate of upward land movement.

Below WAR MEMORIAL, PALMERSTON NORTH

A small South Island town laid first claim to the name Palmerston so the provincial centre of the rich sheep and dairy farming area of Manawatu is Palmerston North. It is a pleasant town with a handsome war memorial and a large university. Massey University was founded in 1926 as an agricultural college and is still New Zealand's pre-eminent learning centre for agricultural sciences.

Over page KAPITI ISLAND

Rugged Kapiti Island, just off the sweeping mainland coast at Paraparaumu, was the stronghold of the 19th-century warrior chief Te Rauparaha. In 1820 the ruthless Ngati Toa chief invaded Kapiti and moved his tribe there from its ancestral home at Kawhia so as to evade a threat from his powerful Waikato neighbours. Te Rauparaha also wanted better access to European whalers and the muskets he could obtain from them. Once armed with muskets his warriors spent the next 20 years marauding up and down New Zealand, killing many thousands of people. The 10-kilometre-long island is now a wildlife reserve.

Left MAIN STREET, GREYTOWN
Founded in 1854, Greytown was the country's first planned inland town and is noted for the fine examples of Victorian architecture that line the main street. The town, named after Governor Sir George Grey, is also noted as the site of New Zealand's first co-operative dairy factory, founded in 1881.

Below CASTLEPOINT
Maori explorer Kupe is said to have discovered this stunningly wild spot around AD 925 while looking for a giant octopus. He found the octopus in a cave under the rock where the Castlepoint lighthouse now stands, but it was the European explorer James Cook who gave the point its name because of the appearance of the 162 metre-high Castle Rock. A reef of tilted rock that creates a sheltered lagoon at Castlepoint is a popular fishing spot and contains more than 70 species of fossil shells.

above MARTINBOROUGH HOTEL
A once sleepy town south of Greytown, Martinborough has become a hip weekend retreat for Wellingtonians and the centre for Wairarapa tourism. The town boasts several fine restaurants and the Martinborough Hotel, built in 1882 and magnificently restored as an upmarket boutique hotel with an excellent bistro and imaginative menu.

right VINEYARD, MARTINBOROUGH
Martinborough owes its new-found tourist popularity to the region's growing reputation as a producer of boutique wines. While small compared with other New Zealand wine regions – in 2003 the area held 3.8 percent of the national vineyard total – there is nonetheless a wide variety of styles. The region is developing as the natural home of pinot noir but it also produces good sauvignon blanc and chardonnay.

Above PUTANGIRUA PINNACLES

New Zealand has several areas of 'badland erosion' but perhaps the most scenically impressive are the Putangirua Pinnacles in a scenic reserve next to the Haurangi Forest Park in the southern Wairarapa. The erosive power of intense rainfall has carved away soft siltstone but the erosion has been resisted in places by a harder layer in the conglomerate. The pillars can be reached on a streambed trail that begins near the forest park's Te Kopi field centre.

Right NGAWI

On the remote and lonely road to the southern tip of the North Island lies a fishing village that is as archetypal as you could get. The rugged Wairarapa coast at Ngawi is no place to moor boats so the fishermen solve the problem by using bulldozers to pull the fishing fleet out of the water each day.

Right LIGHTHOUSE, CAPE PALLISER
There are 252 steps up to the lighthouse at Cape Palliser, the most southern spot in the North Island. On a clear day it is worth the climb to the light, built in 1897 with views across Cook Strait to the South Island. Cape Palliser also has the North Island's largest seal colony.

Below MEMORIAL, RIMUTUKA RANGE
Special railway engines with an additional wheel that clamped onto a central track were once used to climb over the Rimutuka Range and into Wellington. There is now an 8-kilometre rail tunnel through the Rimutakas but motor traffic must still climb over the windswept summit where there is a memorial to the first European crossing of the range. The old railway incline is now a walking and mountain biking trail.

Left WELLINGTON CITY AND HARBOUR

The New Zealand capital is clustered around the hills of a magnificent natural harbour. The city, on the edge of Cook Strait, is often subject to wind streaming out of the southern oceans. But at its best 'Windy Wellington' is one of the most beautiful cities in the world and a proud capital. Large vehicular ferries cross from Wellington to the South Island several times a day.

Below KELBURN CABLE CAR

The hills that confine Wellington have been the cause of considerable innovation in house design. The steep streets have also resulted in one novel transportation solution. A cable car has carried passengers to the pleasant hillside suburb of Kelburn since 1902.

Above ORIENTAL BAY

Wellington's Oriental Bay has more than a little similarity with cities in the East, such as Hong Kong. The suburb, just minutes from the centre of the city, contains some of the capital's most expensive houses and apartments with boat sheds and yacht moorings at their front door.

Above **PARLIAMENT BUILDINGS**
Three buildings, the Beehive, Old Parliament House and the Parliamentary Library, make up New Zealand's Parliamentary complex. The copper-domed Beehive, which houses the offices of the executive, was designed by British architect Sir Basil Spence and completed in 1980 after 11, often controversial, years in the making. Parliament House, built in 1922, has recently had a major renovation.

Right **WELLINGTON RAILWAY STATION**
The massive classical frontage of Wellington's Railway Station, with its eight Doric columns, provides a symbolic gateway to the city. Work began on the station in 1933 and it opened in June 1937, housing the railway terminal and the offices of the Railway Department. It is a building of grand proportions, with floor space originally covering 1.5 hectares with 250 rooms and over a kilometre of corridors.

Above TE PAPA TONGAREWA

Centrepiece of Wellington's redevelopment is the new national museum, Te Papa Tongarewa – Our Place. Opened in 1989, Te Papa is one of the most modern museums in the world, designed to inform visitors about the past and the present and also to entertain. Many of its displays are interactive. An exhibition devoted to the movie trilogy 'Lord of the Rings', filmed in New Zealand, was held in 2003.

Below WESTPAC TRUST STADIUM

Wellington built its new stadium right in the heart of the city on land left vacant by port redevelopment. It was designed so spectators would be close to the onfield action in a circular style that soon led it to be dubbed The Cake Tin. Officially the Westpac Trust Stadium, the venue is used for rugby and international cricket.

Below PETONE WHARF

While there is no shortage of foreshore in the harbour-based city, the capital is not renowned for its beaches. Nonetheless, the drive to the seaside suburb of Eastbourne, past the Petone Wharf and the Petone foreshore, is a delight, particularly at dawn. There is a memorial on the Petone seafront to mark the landing of Wellington's first European settlers in 1839.

THE SOUTH

ISLAND

Previous pages PUNAKAIKI
The 30,000-hectare Paparoa National Park, New Zealand's 12th when it was opened in 1987, is noted for its coastal scenery, being some of the finest on the South Island's West Coast. The park's top attraction is the Pancake Rocks and Blowholes at Dolomite Point near the small settlement of Punakaiki. The blowholes carved out of the limestone rock perform best at high tide.

Above INTER-ISLAND FERRIES
There are several sailings each day of roll-on, roll-off ferries that link the North and South Islands. The ferries are designed to carry railway wagons, as well as trucks, private vehicles and independent passengers. Tory Channel, where the *Aratere* is passing its fleet-mate the *Arahura*, is the entrance to the sounds.

Below PICTON
Picton, at the head of Queen Charlotte Sound in the Marlborough Sounds, is the destination for ferries from the North Island. The small port bustles when the ferry is in but is sleepy at other times, especially in winter. The ferry trip through Tory Channel and up Queen Charlotte Sound is an attraction in itself, giving visitors an introduction to the intricate waterways with their numerous coves, bays and islands.

Right MARLBOROUGH SOUNDS
Even in the evening light the 1203-metre summit of Mt Stokes provides a commanding vantage point across the Marlborough Sounds Arapawa Island and Cook Strait to the Wellington coast on the North Island. From the summit of Arapawa Island Captain Cook discovered that the 'eastern sea' (the Pacific) was connected to the 'western sea' (the Tasman) by a broad strait, which today carries his name.

Right **MARLBOROUGH WINERY**
Floral sauvignon blancs from the Marlborough region, the largest wine-producing area in New Zealand, have an outstanding international reputation. Marlborough chardonnays and fruity rieslings are also highly ranked. The Allan Scott winery regularly produces medal-winning wines.

Below **WAIRAU VALLEY**
Conflict over dubious land sales on the Wairau Plains and Wairau Valley, near Blenheim, caused a fatal confrontation between the warrior chief Te Rauparaha and the land buyers of the New Zealand Company in 1843. A skirmish precipitated by a party of armed Europeans ended with 22 of the party dead and is known as the Wairau Affray. The braided Wairau River is an excellent trout fishery.

Right **BLENHEIM RAILWAY STATION**
The largest town in the Marlborough region, Blenheim lies south of Picton on the Wairau Plains, at the centre of the country's best-known wine-growing district. Blenheim's historic railway station buildings are well preserved, although they have been relocated a short distance. They now house the Marlborough Information and Travel Centre.

Below **WAIRAU PLAINS**
The flat Wairau farmland has been variously used for horticulture and sheep and cattle grazing. The valley seems nicely sheltered by the Richmond Range but therein lies a major problem for agriculture that seems to be getting worse. The precipitation in the prevailing westerlies is mostly caught by the ranges, leaving the Wairau pastures in their lee prone to extreme drought.

Right **TOTARANUI**
The golden sweep of beach at Totaranui marks
the end of the Coast Track in the Abel Tasman
National Park. The 22,139-hectare park tucked
into the north-western tip of the South Island is
New Zealand's smallest but it is also the most
popular with about 30,000 people every year
walking the three-day trail, one of New
Zealand's Great Walks. The coast is also a
popular sea kayaking venue.

Left **TONGA BEACH**
The sands of Tonga Beach and other coves
along the Abel Tasman coastline have become
a New Zealand icon. Quartz and marble eroded
to a glistening honey-coloured sugar sparkles in
the sunlight, a soft, beguiling border between
the green hills of regenerating native bush and
a turquoise sea of clearest water. In places it
evokes an image of the tropics and coral atolls
except that fur seals laze on the rocky
foreshore of Tonga Island.

BARK BAY

he first Europeans to settle at the Bark Bay
et, Timothy Huffman and his four sons, made
ving by collecting large amounts of bark
m rimu and beech trees and shipping it to
lson tanneries where it was used to tan
des. The family left in 1904 but walkers on
e Abel Tasman Coast Track can stay
ernight at a 28-bunk Department of
onservation hut built on the site of the
uffman's old Bark Bay homestead.

WHARARIKI BEACH

harariki Beach, 29 kilometres north of the
olden Bay township of Collingwood, is a
unning introduction to the wild West Coast.
 rocky islets and archways are reached by a
ort walk across the dunes from the carpark
 Puponga at the bottom of Farewell Spit. You
ay be greeted by fur seals here.

Above **FAREWELL SPIT**
Farewell Spit, the 26 kilometre-long finger of sand dunes, shell banks and marshland that encloses Golden Bay on the north-western tip of the South Island, is an internationally important wetland and bird sanctuary that is the summer home to thousands of birds that have migrated from the Arctic tundra. The spit was named by Captain Cook when leaving New Zealand in 1770.

Right **PILLAR POINT**
During the Second World War a radar station and navigation light were sited at Pillar Point at the base of Farewell Spit. It used to be a steep 30-minute climb to the views over the Tasman Sea but 4WD tours to nearby Cape Farewell usually include a visit to Pillar Point and its sandstone bluffs and archways. The Cape is a place of cliffs and fierce winds but it is also home to a seal colony.

Left **HARWOOD'S HOLE**
The biggest drop shaft and cave entrance in the southern hemisphere is found amongst the weathered limestone near Takaka Hill, which lies between Tasman Bay and Golden Bay. Over 370 metres deep, the hole features a 183-metre vertical drop. Experienced cavers abseil into the cave system, created by rivers that have long since disappeared underground, and emerge at Gorge Creek.

Below **WAIKOROPUPU SPRINGS**
Waikoropupu Springs, near Takaka, are the largest springs in New Zealand and are renowned for the clarity of their water. Commonly known as Pupu Springs, they contain two large vents that send stones 'dancing' upwards with the force of water, and several smaller vents that make sand dance. The clear, cold water is slightly salty but it is believed the springs are fed by the Takaka River and a stream that runs underground below Harwood's Hole.

Left **BULLER GORGE**
The spectacular Buller Gorge, with its mist-shrouded forests, still bears the scars of slips and land deformation caused by major earthquakes in 1929 and 1968. The most notable section of this route from Nelson to the West Coast is the narrow Hawks Crag cutting where the road has been blasted into the cliff-face beside the Buller River. The crag is named after an early gold prospector.

Below **HEAPHY TRACK**
The 77-kilometre Heaphy Track from Aorere, near Collingwood, to Kohaihai on the West Coast is one of New Zealand's Great Walks. The trail, which goes from the ranges of the Kahurangi National Park to West Coast beaches, takes four to six days to traverse. It includes many river and stream crossings but some have swingbridges provided, such as at Wekakura Creek. The track is named after Major Charles Heaphy, who was awarded the Victoria Cross during the Waikato Land Wars in 1864.

Above COAST, HEAPHY TRACK
A feature of the Heaphy Track is the coastal
section from the mouth of the Heaphy River to
the Kohaihai River. The trail is an energy-
sapping mix of trudging through sand, boulder
hopping, stream crossing and walking through
the bush fringe - the very features that give the
Heaphy its character. The coast is not
recommended for swimming.

Right NIKAU, HEAPHY TRACK
In spring, the enormous nikau palm groves that
clothe the coastal backdrop to the Heaphy
Track are broken by vibrant flashes of rata trees
in flower. The nikau is unique as the most
southern growing palm in the world and New
Zealand's only indigenous palm species. It is
found in coastal, lowland and hilly forests in the
North Island and around the top of the South
Island. The nikau's stately fronds give the forest
a distinctly subtropical appearance.

Right **MARUIA SPRINGS**
At Maruia Springs, near Lewis Pass on the highway to Westport, natural hot springs are pumped into outdoor rock pools and a Japanese-style bathhouse. The springs are perhaps best enjoyed in winter when snowflakes may softly fall on bathers relaxing in the warm water.

Left PAPAROA NATIONAL PARK
Paparoa earned its National Park status because of the stunning limestone formations of the region, both inland and on the coast. The limestone bluffs that tower above Fox River have been sculpted by centuries of exposure to the weather. On the coast at Punakaiki the outcrops of stratified limestone have formed the distinctive Pancake Rocks at Dolomite Point and several spectacular blowholes.

Above DAIRY COWS, GREYMOUTH
The West Coast is noted for its torrential rainfall – around 5 metres a year as the prevailing westerly weather hits the mountains of the Southern Alps. Yet even 'Wetland', as some unkind people call the Coast, gets a fair dose of sunshine, as much, in fact as Christchurch. That means this dairy herd near Greymouth can enjoy both lush grass and sunshine.

Left MEMORIAL CLOCK, HOKITIKA
In the 1860s Hokitika was a gold mining boom town with a population of more than 6000 and one of the busiest ports in the country. Ships regularly ran aground or were wrecked in the treacherous river bar. The town happily survives without half of its former population as a slightly eccentric centre, rich in history and natural recreation resources. The memorial clock in the main street was built in 1901–02 to commemorate the Boer War and King Edward VII's coronation.

Below BIG SANDFLY, PUKEKURA
Many who have ventured into the Westland bush would suggest that the giant sandfly sculpture at the Bushman's Centre in Pukekura is no exaggeration. Famed early explorer Charlie Douglas went so far as to suggest that if a town was formed at the mouth of the Cascade River it should be called Sandfly. 'At the first streak of day he [the sandfly] proceeds to business with a fiendish skill,' wrote the whimsical Douglas.

Above OKARITO LAGOON
A colony of the rare and beautiful white heron, the kotuku, which nest in the rimu tree tops at the Waitangiroto sanctuary at Okarito Lagoon, have ensured protection for the lagoon and tidal flats, the largest unmodified wetland in New Zealand. The kotuku, with a population that never rises above around 100 birds, breeds in New Zealand only at Okarito before dispersing to wetlands and estuaries throughout the country. Royal spoonbills also breed at the site.

Right and overleaf LAKE MATHESON
Lake Matheson near Fox Glacier township in Westland National Park is perhaps the most photographed stretch of water in New Zealand. The bush-fringed lake is in sand country on the road to Gillespie's Beach. In the early morning and evening the calm, dark waters of the lake mirror a stunning panorama of the Southern Alps giants of Aoraki/Mt Cook and Mt Tasman. A short walk around the lake reveals the picture postcard reflections.

Above FRANZ JOSEF

Franz Joseph township sits beneath the Franz Josef Glacier, one of the two mighty glaciers of Westland National Park that tumble out of the Southern Alps almost to the shores of the Tasman Sea. There is a National Park visitors' centre at Franz Josef, as well as a range of accommodation.

Left WELCOME FLAT POOLS

The natural hot pools at Welcome Flat in the Copland Valley, South Westland, are indeed welcomed by trampers and climbers who have made the arduous Copland Pass crossing over the Southern Alps. A modern Department of Conservation hut at Welcome Flat sleeps 40.

Above **FRANZ JOSEF GLACIER**
Austrian explorer Julius Haast named the glacier after the Austrian emperor. The glacier has generally been in retreat since Haast named it in 1865 until beginning a rapid advance in 1985. While the terminal is still some kilometres back from where Haast first recorded it, the river of ice has been moving around 70 centimetres a day. An excellent viewing spot is from the Sentinel Rock lookout.

Left **COPLAND VALLEY**
An easier way to reach the hot springs at Welcome Flat than by climbing over the Alps is to take a pleasant six-hour walk up the Copland Valley. The track, which starts along the highway to Haast, includes this historic swingbridge. The Copland Pass should not be attempted by walkers unless accompanied by a professional mountain guide.

Above ALBERT GLACIER

The névé (uncompressed snow) at the head of the Albert Glacier, a vast snowfield between the Fox Range and Pioneer Ridge in Westland National Park, makes for superb ski touring using Pioneer Hut, a remote mountain hut, as a base. Mt Tasman, the second highest peak in New Zealand, provides the backdrop to the Albert, which feeds its ice into the Fox Glacier.

Left and right FOX GLACIER

Fox Glacier, given its name in 1872 after a visit by the New Zealand Prime Minister, Sir William Fox, has also been galloping forward over the last 20 years, although the rate of advance is not as dramatic as with the Franz Josef. The glacier, over 13 kilometres long, descends steeply from 2750 metres above sea level to 245 metres.

t WAIAU RIVER
e bridge across the Waiau River near
anmer Springs was built in 1886 to replace
e original wooden bridge that blew down in
e 1870s. After the thermal springs were
scovered by Europeans in 1859, Hanmer was
veloped as a health spa. It remains a lively
urism centre.

ght **TEMPLE BASIN SKIFIELD**
he Temple Basin Skifield in Arthur's Pass
ational Park is one of a dozen in New Zealand
at are run by ski clubs. Most have on-field
ccommodation in club huts and while the lift
quipment may be fairly basic, the cost of club
eld skiing is considerably less than on
ommercial ski areas.

eft and right **OTIRA GORGE**
he modern Otira Viaduct has made road travel
ver the Otira River and through the Otira
orge to Arthur's Pass much easier than of old.
ut the rail line, which roughly runs parallel with
he road, has had it much easier for decades.
n 8.5-kilometre tunnel runs through the
outhern Alps between Otira and Arthur's
ass. The tunnel was started from both ends in
908 and when the tunnellers met under the
ountains the alignment was just 25
illimetres out. The tunnel was completed in
923 and is on the route of the TranzAlpine, the
opular train journey across the South Island
rom Christchurch to Greymouth. One thing
hat remains unchanged in the Otira Gorge is
he brilliance of the rata trees flowering on the
illsides.

Above and left KAIKOURA
Kaikoura, on the east coast south of
Marlborough, means 'meal of crayfish'. Fresh
crayfish or rock lobster is still readily available in
the region, including from outlets such as the
well-known roadside stall Nin's Bin. Sea life is
at the heart of Kaikoura's economy, with fishing
and, more recently, tourism providing income.
The coast has become internationally
renowned for whale watching and swimming
with dolphins. Also seen on carefully controlled
marine mammal-watching tours are orca, fur
seals and pilot whales, minke, humpback and
southern right.

Above SEAWARD KAIKOURAS
The Kaikoura Peninsula, with its snow-covered backdrop of the Seaward Kaikoura Range, has changed from a sleepy fishing region into a bustling tourism centre. Sperm whales frequent the deep ocean trench just off the Kaikoura coast where the water plunges to more than 00 metres. Warm and cold currents converge, bringing krill and other whale food to the surface.

Left ROCK ART, KAIKOURA
There may be little but wildlife watching to do at Kaikoura but when the weather puts a stop to whale or dolphin watching young backpacking tourists kill time constructively. At Goose Bay, one of the preferred dolphin-watching locations, visitors have started a tradition of rock art.

Right **TIMEBALL TOWER, LYTTELTON**
The ornate Timeball Station above Lyttelton Harbour was built in 1876 as an aid to shipping. Ships in the harbour were able to set their chronometers by the huge ball that was hoisted to the top of a mast on the roof of the tower and dropped each day, for 58 years, at precisely 1 pm Greenwich Mean Time.

Below **GODLEY HEAD**
Godley Head at the entrance to Lyttelton Harbour points like a finger back towards the city of Christchurch and the seaside suburb of Sumner. A tunnel under the Port Hills links Christchurch with Lyttelton, which serves as the city's port. The harbour, on Banks Peninsula, is situated within the eroded remnant of a massive extinct volcano.

Above and left **AKAROA**
Akaroa, a harbour and small town on the south of Banks Peninsula, is a historical oddity. The town, 82 kilometres from Christchurch, was established by 63 French settlers in 1840 and despite British claims of sovereignty they retained many French connections. At Duvauchelle at the head of the harbour there is an old post office that looks much the same as when first built. Streets and houses in Akaroa have French names and descendants of the original French settlers still live in the town. Rue Lavaud is the main street.

Over page **BANKS PENINSULA**
One of the few mapping errors that Captain Cook made was to consider Banks Peninsula an island when he named it after his botanist, Sir Joseph Banks. It was left to a later generation of seafarers to alter the name. Ironically, Cook's surmise wasn't too far off the mark. The Peninsula is essentially a huge volcanic island that grew out of the sea. Over millions of years erosion from the Southern Alps formed the Canterbury Plains and turned Banks Island into Banks Peninsula.

ft AVON RIVER

hen a river runs through a new city in the
outh Pacific being modelled on Olde England,
hat other name to give it but the Avon? The
ver is a delight to walk along or row down. At
e old Antigua boatsheds you can hire canoes
r rowboats, or relax in a punt while someone
se does the work.

ght and below CATHEDRAL SQUARE

o other New Zealand city has a heart as
early defined as Cathedral Square in
hristchurch. The square is dominated by the
nglican Cathedral, consecrated in 1881, and
s 63-metre spire, but it is also the site of new
ndmarks, such as the eccentric Wizard, a
oap box orator, and the modern chalice
culpture by Neil Dawson. The Square is also a
najor tourist draw for a city often described as
e most English in New Zealand. Founded in
850 under the auspices of the Church of
ngland, Christchurch displays orderly
ettlement, bounteous gardens and English
treet names. While the city may have
utgrown its pious beginnings, it still retains
nuch of its defining character.

Below CHRISTCHURCH TRAMS

Trams carried commuters along Christchurch
streets for 60 years after first being introduced
in 1905. Modern Christchurch has
reconstructed a 2.5-kilometre tram loop around
many of the city's best tourism features and
shopping areas and restored green and cream
trams again rumble around the city centre.

Above OMARAMA

Omarama is in the heart of many high-country sheep stations that carry huge flocks of fine-wool merinos. But the town would likely be little more than a truck stop on the highway south if it were not for the fine trout fishing in the rivers and hydro lakes of the Waitaki Valley and the peculiarity of its location – in a heat bowl adjoining the foothills of the Southern Alps. The north-west thermal currents that soar out of the valley have made Omarama an internationally recognised gliding centre.

Right BIG SALMON, RAKAIA

The giant salmon statue on the outskirts of Rakaia boasts of the good fishing in the Rakaia River. Wild salmon run up several of the braided rivers of South Canterbury, providing top sport for anglers, particularly at the river mouths. The Rakaia Gorge on the Rakaia River is the destination for popular jet boat jaunts.

Above **ROCK DRAWINGS, TAKIROA**
At Takiroa, 50 kilometres west of Oamaru, sheltered sandstone cliffs have been used as a canvas for ochre and charcoal drawings. It is believed that the primitive art, discovered in 1852, possibly symbolises humans and taniwha (water monsters) and dates from the moa-hunting era around the 10th to 12th centuries AD. There are other rock art sites on private land.

Left **MUSEUM, GERALDINE**
Geraldine, founded in 1854 when surveyor Samuel Hewlings built the first home in the town, is a pretty place tucked into the hills of the Mackenzie Country. The town is filled with shady trees that are peacefully green in summer and beautifully golden in the autumn. The town's historic buildings include the old town board office, now used as a museum.

Left SHEEPDOG STATUE, LAKE TEKAPO

The Mackenzie Country takes its name (albeit with a slightly different spelling) from a Scottish shepherd, James Mckenzie, who made a living droving sheep in Canterbury and Otago. In 1855 the penniless Highlander got permission to farm the empty tussock grasslands of the Mackenzie Basin but, with the help of his well-trained collie dog, stocked the land with another runholder's sheep. Mckenzie was arrested and sentenced to five years in jail but he was pardoned after nine months and deported.

Right MUSTER, MACKENZIE COUNTR

The hills of the Mackenzie Country do not seem particularly good for grazing but merino sheep thrive here. The fine-wool breed can withstand the heat of summer when temperatures are often above 30 degrees Celsius, yet still happily cope with winter snows.

Below CHURCH OF THE GOOD SHEPHERD

The Church of the Good Shepherd on the shores of Lake Tekapo is likely the most photographed church in the country. Built from stone and oak timber in 1935, it is framed by the alpine setting of the snow-capped Two Thumb Range.

Previous pages LAKE PUKAKI
Aoraki/Mt Cook pokes its 3754-metre summit above the clouds. The snows of the highest mountain in New Zealand feed the Tasman Glacier which, when joined by the ice melt of the Hooker River, becomes the Tasman River before flowing into Lake Pukaki. The glacier-fed lake is thick with suspended 'glacial flour', finely ground rock debris created by moving ice, which gives the water a distinctive pale blue colour.

Right AORAKI/MT COOK
On Christmas Day 1894 three young New Zealanders, Tom Fyfe, George Graham and Jack Clarke, beat a queue of European challengers and reached the top of New Zealand's highest mountain. Aoraki/Mt Cook has since been climbed by many hundreds of people, but it remains a daunting mountaineering challenge and some faces were only climbed in the late 20th century.

Above HOOKER VALLEY
The Hooker Valley and Glacier to the west of the Mt Cook Range gives access to many of the highest peaks on the Main Divide as well as to the Copland Pass crossing over the Southern Alps. Ice melt from the Hooker drains into the Mueller Glacier terminal lake (before exiting into the Hooker River). The lake, as seen from a track on the Sealy Range, is big enough for a visitor to be offered the chance to kayak among its icebergs.

Right AHURIRI RIVER
The Ahuriri River, flowing into Lake Benmore near Omarama, is a trout fishery of national importance, its waters especially protected by a Water Conservation Order. The upper reaches are also where trophy trout await the attention of experienced anglers.

Left CLAY CLIFFS, OMARAMA
The Clay Cliffs above the Ahuriri River near Omarama are a classic example of badland erosion, continually weathered over time to give the appearance of a giant fossilised pine forest. The clay and gravel cliffs have been formed by land being pushed up along the active Osler fault line, and weathered into pinnacles.

Above QUEENSTOWN

Queenstown, the jewel of the south, is New Zealand's most famous tourist town. It is set in a scenically stunning alpine location on the shores of Lake Wakatipu. The Remarkable Range to the east is Queenstown's most distinctive backdrop while Bobs Peak, reached by gondola from almost in the town centre, gives photographers panoramic frames.

Right WILLIAM REES

Modern Queenstown is devoted to tourism but it wasn't always so. The town has its origins in sheep and gold. William Gilbert Rees, whose statue stands on the Queenstown waterfront, was the first of the sheepmen settlers in the area and the founder of the town. The focus of the town changed in 1862 when two shearers, Thomas Arthur and Harry Redfern, discovered gold on the banks of the Shotover River. Now the gold comes from tourist dollars – and most sheep stations are still thriving.

Right BUNGY, KAWARAU RIVER

The world's first-ever commercial bungy jump site was established by A.J. Hackett in 1986 on the Kawarau Suspension Bridge, 23 kilometres from Queenstown. The 43-metre plunge over the Kawarau River is no longer the longest bungy drop in the world – you can drop 71 metres into the Shotover River gorge and 102 metres into Skippers Canyon – but the Kawarau jump remains the most popular in the region.

Below TSS EARNSLAW

The stately steel-hulled TSS *Earnslaw* has been plying the waters of Lake Wakatipu since 1912. The coal-fired twin-screw steamship was built in Dunedin, completely dismantled and railed to Kingston where it was reassembled and launched. When its daily run between Kingston and Queenstown was stopped in 1969 – the vessel could carry more than 800 passengers at 13 knots – the *Earnslaw* was splendidly restored and its brass tubes polished for tourist cruises on Wakatipu.

Right GLENORCHY

Until a road was completed in 1962, Glenorchy, at the head of Lake Wakatipu, could only be reached by steamers such as the TSS *Earnslaw*. People, freight, runholders' stock and bales of wool were all shipped to and from the far reaches of the lake. Glenorchy is the starting point for many major tracks including the Routeburn and the Rees-Dart, but the days have gone when homebound trampers could dry their gear on the boilers of the *Earnslaw*.

Below KINGSTON FLYER

The Kingston Flyer, a restored coal-fired locomotive and vintage carriages dating from the early 1900s, steams daily on a 14-kilometre stretch of track between Kingston and Fairlight on the southern shores of Lake Wakatipu. The original Kingston Flyer was operated between Kingston and the Main South Line at Gore until the mid-1950s.

Above ROUTEBURN WALK

The Routeburn Track in Mt Aspiring National Park is often found in international lists of the world's great walks. The track begins on the Routeburn River Flats before climbing over the Humboldt Mountains and down to the Hollyford River. Even in summer there may be snow on the trail, which follows an old Maori route across the Alps to South Westland, and the area is prone to sudden weather change.

Right ARROWTOWN

Painters love to paint Arrowtown. The tiny township, situated not far from the Coronet Peak skifield near Queenstown, began life as a gold mining town. Now around 60 of the 19th-century wooden buildings that line its main street have been restored. And in the autumn a beautiful avenue of deciduous trees turn as golden as the metal that first gave the town life.

Previous pages MT ASPIRING
Mt Aspiring is the New Zealand Matterhorn, a
'lofty conical peak', as surveyor J.T. Thomson
noted in his fieldbook in 1857 when he named
the mountain. Maori called it Tititea, glittering
peak, and other than the high mountains in the
Aoraki/Mt Cook region, 50 kilometres to the
north, it is unchallenged in southern New
Zealand. Aspiring is like a four-sided pyramid
with the flanks leading to the Bonar (right),
Therma and Volta glaciers. Mt Avalanche is a
smaller outlying peak.

Right CARDRONA HOTEL
The Cardrona Hotel is surely the most
recognisable in New Zealand. Its facade
features regularly in advertisements in
magazines and on television on any subject
that wants to create the atmosphere of the
19th-century Otago goldfields or the manly
shepherds of high-country sheep stations. The
hotel in the Cardrona Valley between Wanaka
and Queenstown has become even more
popular since the sealing of the Crown Range
Road and is a well-visited watering hole for
skiers at the Cardrona Ski Resort.

Above LAKE WANAKA

Lake Wanaka and the township of Wanaka are near neighbours and major rivals to Queenstown for the hearts and dollars of tourists. The area was once almost a private holiday playground for the people of Otago, but not any more. Two skifields, a lake that is an excellent trout fishery, a fledgling wine industry and stunning scenery are good reason for others to visit too.

Left LINDIS PASS

The light playing on the tussock-clad hills of the Lindis Pass has drawn the attention of many artists, particularly those using print wash techniques. Throughout the day the pattern of shadow and highlights in the convoluted hillsides is forever changing.

Above and below CROMWELL

You might say that Cromwell, a former central Otago gold-mining town, has had its ups and downs. It moved from gold to stone fruit, its alluvial soil and climate of hot summers and cold winters producing legendary apricots, peaches and pears. And then a nation demanded more electricity and in 1992 many of the orchards and parts of Cromwell itself were drowned by the creation of Lake Dunstan. Fortunately, not all was lost. A number of old buildings were relocated to what is now Old Cromwell Town. And the region retains its link with fruit in orchards that survived the flooding and in giant sculpture.

Right **CLYDE**
Clyde, once the centre of the Dunstan
goldfields, is lined with stone buildings dating
back to the 1860s. The town has two
museums, one depicting domestic life on the
goldfields, the other a display of the machinery
used to extract the precious metal, but Clyde
now lives in the shadow of the Clyde Dam.

Below **CLYDE DAM**
The 432-metre-high Clyde Dam across the
Clutha River at Cromwell Gorge has a
controversial history. The Clutha River, which
discharges the largest volume of water of any
in New Zealand, powers several hydro-electric
stations but the Clyde Dam prompted
environmental protest because of the amount
of land that would have been submerged by
the lake behind it. A compromise was reached
and the final dam was lower than one of the
earlier proposals.

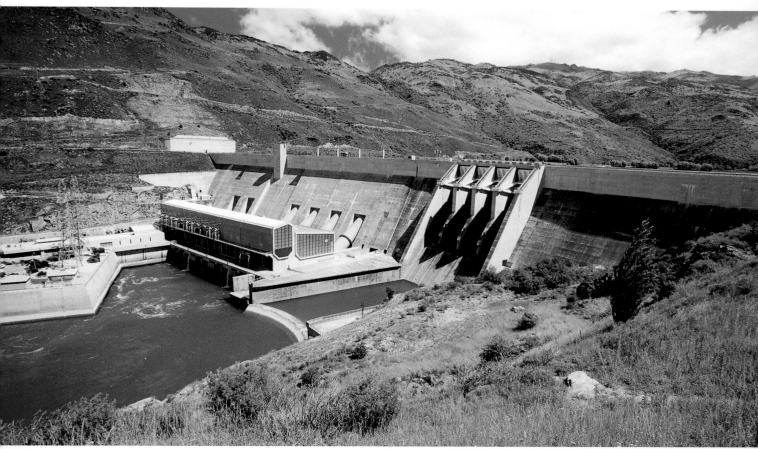

Right OAMARU

Refrigerated shipping made Oamaru
prosperous by providing a way to get mutton to
cooks in Europe. But the enduring signature of
the town is its stone that has provided the base
material for many of New Zealand's stately
buildings, including the city's Post Office, built
in 1883, and the war memorial.

Below MOERAKI BOULDERS

The large spherical boulders scattered along
the beach at Moeraki, 30 kilometres south of
Oamaru, are about 60 million years old. Maori
believe they are baskets, gourds and kumara
washed ashore from a canoe wrecked near
Shag Point. Modern science explains them as
concretions formed over four million years
around a central limestone core and now
washed from the shoreline bluffs. Two of the
boulders contain fossilised dinosaur bones.

Left OAMARU BANKS
Oamaru stone was the natural, solid material chosen to build the Bank of Otago (1871) and the Bank of New South Wales (1883) in Oamaru. There are 22 classified historic buildings in the town, many using the local limestone which when mined is soft enough to be sawn but when exposed to the air hardens as an enduring building material.

Left OTAGO UNIVERSITY

Dunedin prides itself as a university town and i recent years there is some reason to suggest that Otago University is the biggest industry in the southern city. The university, founded in 1869 with just 81 students and the first in New Zealand, now attracts students from throughout the country and around the world.

Below OCTAGON, DUNEDIN

Dunedin, Celtic for Edinburgh, is the South Island's second city. It was founded by Scottish settlers and during the days of the Otago gold rush was the largest city in New Zealand. As befits its heritage the Octagon in the centre of Dunedin has a Town Hall, a Cathedral – and a statue to poet Robert Burns.

ROBERT BURNS
25 JANUARY 1759
1796

Above **LARNACH CASTLE**
The best-known building on the Otago Peninsula is Larnach Castle, built by William Larnach in 1871. It is an extravagant mixture of architectural styles, a symbol of the wealth of early Dunedin and cost a fortune to build. Larnach, a merchant and politician, committed suicide at Parliament House in 1898.

Left **DUNEDIN RAILWAY STATION**
The ostentatious wealth of Dunedin towards the end of the 19th century resulted in several grand buildings. The Railway Station was built in Flemish Renaissance style of basalt with Oamaru limestone facings. The building, completed in 1906, features copper – domed towers, lions perched on the clock tower and elaborate stonework around the arched windows. Its designer was knighted.

Over page **NUGGET POINT**
Seals often come ashore beneath the Nugget Point lighthouse, built in 1869, on the Catlins coast. The Catlins, which stretches from Waipapa Point in Southland to Nugget Point in South Otago, is an area noted for its southern ocean wildlife. The rocks below the stone lighthouse are the only place on mainland New Zealand where Hooker's sealions co-exist with elephant seals.

Left SOUTHLAND MUSEUM
The Southland Museum and Art Gallery in Invercargill is noted for its exhibits on New Zealand's subantarctic islands. Its other noted attraction is a house devoted to New Zealand reptiles and home to several exceptionally old tuatara, a lizard species that dates back to the days of the dinosaurs. A bronze statue of a tuatara fronts the reptile house.

Right WATER TOWER, INVERCARGILL
Invercargill has taken a new lease of life since many people in the rest of the country discovered just how cheap it could be to live in a town that most considered an old-fashioned backwater. The infrastructure doesn't change, however. No amount of modern money could construct the 27.43-metre Victorian-style brick water tower built in 1889.

Below TOWN HALL
The historic buildings of Invercargill include the city's Town Hall. Southland was initially dismissed by European settlers as nothing more than bogland. But it prospered from the logging of its rimu forests and is now a major centre for dairy farming, with relatively cheap land – and plenty of rain for grass growth.

Left BIG TROUT, GORE
Southland locals may boast many claims to fame but one on which there can be little argument is the quality of its brown trout fishery, particularly in the Mataura River. The Mataura attracts anglers from around the world but besides the Mataura the region boasts 150 kilometres of other trout waters. Gore, between Invercargill and Dunedin, prides itself as the brown trout capital of the world.

Right STIRLING POINT, BLUFF
'From North Cape to Bluff' usually denotes the length you can travel in New Zealand. At Stirling Point on the eastern headland of the Bluff Peninsula is a sign to indicate the end of State Highway 1, the road that began at Cape Reinga in the North Island. The sign shows the distances to the South Pole and elsewhere in the world.

Below PAUA HOUSE, BLUFF
As befits a place at the end of the land, Bluff has its eccentrics. The couple who decorated their home with paua shells could be described as such. But paua, or abalone, is a prized seafood and the shell is used for jewellery – so why not decorate a house with it?

Above BIG TAKAHE, TE ANAU
The takahe, a flightless bird, was thought to be extinct until a small colony was discovered in Fiordland in 1948. The species remain 200 survivors but major efforts at various predator-free sanctuaries are being made to breed a viable population. At the Department of Conservation's wildlife centre at Te Anau, one of the breeding centres is fronted by a giant model of the rare bird.

Right MILFORD TRACK
The 54-kilometre Milford Track, which crosses the Southern Alps from Lake Te Anau to Milford Sound, is grandly proclaimed as the finest walk in the world. That may be a touch parochial but the track is certainly one of the world's great walking experiences and each year feels the boots of thousands of trekkers, many from overseas.

Right MACKINNON PASS
Quintin Mackinnon, the first European to find a viable route to Milford in 1888, leaves his name on the Mackinnon Pass. For all its beauty, especially when the Mt Cook lilies are in flower, the pass is an alpine route that demands caution. The lilies are actually a species of buttercup.

Over page MILFORD SOUND
Milford Sound is one of New Zealand's most famous tourist destinations. The 22-kilometre-long fiord that opens to the Tasman Sea is dominated by the 1695-metre Mitre Peak and surrounded by other sheer peaks that are usually decorated with ribbons of waterfalls. The falls are not surprising, given that an average of 5.5 metres of rain is deposited on the area each year.

First published in 2003 by New Holland Publishers (NZ) Ltd
Auckland • Sydney • London • Cape Town

218 Lake Road, Northcote, Auckland, New Zealand
14 Aquatic Drive, Frenchs Forest, NSW 2086, Australia
86-88 Edgware Road, London W2 2EA, United Kingdom
80 McKenzie Street, Cape Town 8001, South Africa

www.newhollandpublishers.co.nz

Copyright (c) 2003 in photography: Rob Suisted
                              www.naturespic.com
Copyright (c) 2003 in text: Colin Moore
Copyright (c) 2003 in maps: New Holland Publishers (NZ) Ltd
Copyright (c) 2003 New Holland Publishers (NZ) Ltd

ISBN: 1 86966 032 3

Publishing manager: Renée Lang
Design: Trevor Newman
Editor: Brian O'Flaherty

A catalogue record for this book is available from
the National Library of New Zealand.

10 9 8 7 6 5 4 3 2

Colour reproduction by Pica Digital Pte Ltd, Singapore
Printed in China through Colorcraft Ltd, Hong Kong

Page 1: 'The Spirit of Napier', Napier, Hawke's Bay

Page 2-3: Whare Waka (canoe house),
Waitangi National Reserve, Bay of Islands

Page 5: Mt Ngauruhoe, Tongariro National Park

Page 6: Chalice sculpture, Cathedral Square, Christchurch

Page 7: Giant artificial fruit, Cromwell, Central Otago